FREUDIAN CONCEPTS IN AMERICA:

THE ROLE OF PSYCHICAL RESEARCH IN PREPARING THE WAY: 1904-1934

Robert Charles Powell

North Charleston, SC:
CreateSpace Independent Publishing Platform, 2015
Copyright © 2015
Robert Charles Powell

ISBN-10: 1511629800
ISBN-13: 978-1511629805

First Edition: April 2015
10 9 8 7 6 5 4 3 2 1

PART ONE – page 3

James Hervey Hyslop (1854-1920) and
the American Institute for Scientific Research,
1904-1934:
An Attempt toward the Coordinated Study of
Psychopathology and Psychical Phenomena
[revised & updated]

PART TWO – page 23

The "Subliminal" versus the "Subconscious" in
the American Acceptance of Psychoanalysis,
1906-1910
[revised & updated]

PART ONE

James Hervey Hyslop (1854-1920) and the American Institute for Scientific Research, 1904-1934: An Attempt toward the Coordinated Study of Psychopathology and Psychical Phenomena

Insofar as Frederic W. H. Myers' conceptions of paranoia – which he called "spirit obsession" – were spread by the Manhattan-based "American Institute for Scientific Research" (1904-1934) – they probably did more to help than to hinder American acceptance of psychodynamic psychotherapy. Certainly, the alternative, primarily neuroanatomic, explanations were less elegant, less comprehensive, and not necessarily more scientific.

[page 161 in the original:] Neither James Hervey Hyslop (1854-1920) nor the American Institute for Scientific Research has commanded much attention in the standard histories of science, even though Hyslop's literary output was tremendous and his institute claimed a membership of 1,200 by the time of his death. Nonetheless, a brief look at the man and his institution might help us grasp some aspects of the nature of American scientific thought in the first decades of this century.

First, let's take a look at the Institute, organized in 1904, but not really activated until 1906. An article in the New York Times, June 24, 1906, written by Hyslop himself, announced that the American Institute for Scientific Research would "comprise the whole field of abnormal psychology, including insanity, hallucinations, epilepsy, neurasthenia, hypnotic phenomena, alcoholism, and whatever exceptional mental phenomena of an abnormal type can be found to need investigation, with a view to the adoption of practical measures for their prevention" (Hyslop, 1906a). That is, while the Institute's range would not be as broad and general as its name might imply, its range would indeed "comprise the whole field of psychology". Various letters dating from 1905-1906, and another article by Hyslop published in January 1907, clarified that there were "two fields of investigation" with which the Institute would be "directly and indirectly occupied" (Hyslop, 1905a; 1907a, p.16). "The first may be called Psychopathology, or Abnormal Psychology, and with that it is desired to associate a philanthropic work ..., a clinic, partly a means of giving practical character to the Institute's aims and partly as a means of facilitating scientific research. The second field is popularly known as Psychic Research and may be called Supernormal Psychology" (Hyslop, 1907a, pp.16-17). "Section A" of the Institute, i.e., the clinic, never became formally operative, though its genesis and informal operations for the focus of this article; "Section B" became the American Society for Psychical Research [page 162 in the original:], with Hyslop as secretary-treasurer and as editor of its Proceedings and Journal. The Institute per se dissolved after Hyslop's death, but the clinic and Society lived on.

So who was James Hervey Hyslop, and what was he trying to do? Why did he insist on trying to organize a psychiatric clinic in conjunction with a psychical research society?

Born August, 1854, to a strict "Associate Presbyterian" farm family living just outside Xenia, Ohio, Hyslop was the second-born child of fifteen and grew up as the eldest of eleven living children. Life was as uncompromising as the ultra-conservative family religion, and he knew death at an early age. A twin sister died within months of his birth; another sister died when he was two; yet another sister plus a brother died when he was ten. These events, plus teachings about "the limited number ... who escape hell," left him with what he later called a "serious half-melancholy disposition". At age thirteen he turned to the reading of theology, which was not too unusual considering his past and that there were few other types of books in the home. His mother died when he was fifteen. I include these opening comments, drawn from Hyslop's handwritten autobiography, to emphasize that he was indeed a "serious" and "half-melancholy" young man (Hyslop, 1904; 1905c, p.215; 1908, p.347; Prince, 1920; Hyslop, G., 1950).

Hyslop's third and fourth decades were equally dry. After high school he spent two years at West Geneva College, Northwood, Ohio, a small institution governed by the Reformed Presbyterian sect, and then moved on at age twenty-one to Wooster University, Wooster, Ohio, a less constrictive Presbyterian institution. True to a form already established, however, Hyslop chose to focus his studies narrowly, upon logic and philosophical analysis, under the tutelage of a later reviser of the "Standard Dictionary". He graduated in 1877. Then, following several years of dreary, barely remunerative employment as a teacher in strict schools and small colleges, Hyslop, in 1880, applied his meager savings toward a seventeen-month stay in Europe. Once in London he was plagued with choosing between Edinburgh University, in honor of his father's religious convictions, and the University of Leipsic, in accord with his own developing skepticism and continued interest in philosophical analysis. He chose Leipsic, studying under Wundt, and thereafter found no favor in his father's eyes.

Upon return to the States he filled several reasonable although temporary positions in college teaching, and then won a fellowship to the Johns Hopkins University, where he completed his doctoral studies in one year, receiving the PhD degree in 1887. After a brief tenure first with the Associated Press, then with Bucknell University, Lewisburg, Pennsylvania, he became Professor of Philosophy at Columbia University, New York City, a post he maintained from 1889 to 1902, during which time he wrote extensively on logic and ethics.

These years at the very end of the last century, when Hyslop was in his late forties, are crucial to our story, although only the barest outline of facts is [page 163 in the original:] known. Hyslop married in 1891, soon fathering two daughters and a son. His father died in 1896, but "returned" spiritually three years later as a "communicator" through the well-investigated medium, Mrs. Leonore Piper (Hyslop, 1905c). Hyslop's wife died, rather suddenly, in 1900. While the dates are not certain, Hyslop clearly suffered "nervous prostration" around 1899-1900. On the very first page of his autobiography he speaks of this period as comprising a complete breakdown of his health. It was during this period that Hyslop became a "spiritist," albeit a skeptical one, seeking evidence for survival of human consciousness beyond bodily death.

"Spiritists" of a rigorously scientific bent, as judged by the standards of their time, first banded together as the Society for Psychical Research, founded in London in 1882. Two years later, the analogous American Society was born, with a number of distinguished Ivy League professors as principal members, and with Richard Hodgson of London, as of 1887, as elected, sometime-salaried, secretary. Around 1892 the American Society, by financial necessity, reorganized as a branch of the English group, retaining Hodgson as secretary until his death in 1905. Meanwhile, Hyslop resolved, apparently in 1904, to reestablish an independent American Society, with the object of later merging the American branch with it. Upon Hodgson's death, the American group tottered, but Hyslop secured the parent society's approval to dissolve the dependent branch, and in May 1906 launched the new American Society for Psychical Research, with himself as principal officer, as well as editor of – and primary contributor to – the Society's publications (Hyslop, 1919, pp.33-35).

As mentioned earlier, this new American Society for Psychical Research was legally "Section B" of Hyslop's duly registered American Institute for Scientific Research. At this point we need to step back and examine pre-1906 indications as to Hyslop's purposes before moving on to explore how these developed during the following decades.

Despite the profuseness of Hyslop's writing, his early suggestions about a relationship between the abnormal and the supernormal are few and generally unclear. In 1905, near the end of an over-500-page volume on epistemology and metaphysics, he noted that, "we have to assume abnormal mental and physical conditions as a requisite for any other influence in the physical world (e.g., "a surviving consciousness") than that which is exercised by the normal and subliminal action of the subject" (Hyslop, 1905b, p.490). He went on to hypothesize that "if there are a few exceptional individuals who are so constituted as to be continually conscious of spiritual influences, their minds will be so much drawn out of proper balance as to the things of this world by the confusing presence of another, that they will often be regarded by other men as insane" (p.492). "Whether spiritualism can actually 'prove' itself scientifically," he added skeptically, "I am not competent to decide, but I think the 'phenomena' of abnormal psychology show that it is possible, if consciousness actually survives death …" (p.494). [page 164 in the original:]

In Science and a Future Life, also published in 1905, Hyslop dropped more explicit hints about his interest in retrieving certain psychical phenomena from a materialistic psychiatric interpretation. As he later commented on a case published in that book, "Ever since I came across an incident … of a veridical apparition in the experience of an insane patient, I have been disposed to think that it might be worthwhile to take more careful account of what some insane patients may say" (Hyslop 1910, p.375). While recognizing that the field of the "supernormal" comprises "fraud, delusion, jugglery, hysteria, hallucinations, insanity, secondary personality, somnambulic and hypnotic phenomena, chance coincidence, alleged telepathy and clairvoyance, mediumistic phenomena, and … so-called telekinesis," and that the "residual phenomena having any significance … (are) perhaps comparatively small in quantity," he felt that the few significant incidents still "sufficed to involve serious attention from intelligent men" (Hyslop, 1905c). He pointed out that "messages" from the "spirit world" may be "as irrational and insane … as you please, if only they show the activity of an intelligence independent of the medium's organism" (p.320). He also noted that the rapid movement of thought characteristic of such "messages" is in normal life "a distinctive mark of what we know in delirium and dreams" (p.327). One of this most interesting hypotheses near the end of the book, attempting to bridge the phenomena seen in spiritism and those seen in psychiatry, was that there are certain "latent functions," which we call "subconscious," that "are not necessary for survival in the present world" but that may be "awaiting the stimulus of another environment …". "The subliminal functions of the physical world may become the supraliminal of the ethereal and spiritual world" (p.376). Moreover, he suggested, there were certain "intermediate mental conditions which do not seem to represent a perfect adaptation to either mode of existence, and so to be abnormal to both …" (p.339). Thus, though it might be like looking for a needle in a haystack, Hyslop felt not only justified but compelled to examine the phenomena of insanity for indications of the mechanisms by which supernormal communications might occur.

Sometime in 1906 Hyslop published two more volumes on psychical research, and there is some suggestion that all four of the 1905-1906 volumes were planned, if not written, at once. In Enigmas of Psychical Research, Hyslop argued that the phenomena interpreted as telepathy, i.e., subliminal communication between the minds of two living persons, was not the only way of explaining certain "facts known to abnormal psychology". One of his strongest arguments was that while "materialism must assume that consciousness performs its functions best when the organism is healthy … subliminal actions involve activities when the normal consciousness seems entirely suspended …". He suggested that the more "we refer telepathic action to subliminal actions the more likely we make the theory that subliminal functions do not represent the natural physical world of sense, but are a foresight of a spiritual world toward which the evolution of the human mind is [page 165 in the original:] moving" (Hyslop, 1906b). Hyslop emphasized that "the ultimate test of a spiritistic theory must be (knowledge of) certain psychological processes and their unity …" (p.384). Borderland of Psychical Research pursued these arguments with greater subtlety, focusing on the phenomena of secondary personality, considered on the borderline between normal and abnormal psychology, for what they reveal about "the claims of the supernormal" (Hyslop, 1906c, p.12).

In May of 1906 Hyslop formally activated the American Institute, registered two years earlier, but it was not until June 24th of that year that the public had any direct indication of his plans. Through a signed article in the New York Times he announced, as noted above, that the American Institute for Scientific Research meant to comprise "the whole field of abnormal psychology". He added, however, that "the first and immediate work of the institute will be the reorganization of psychical research in this country ..." (Hyslop, 1906a).

Six months later, in volume one, issue one of the Journal of the American Society for Psychical Research, Hyslop was more specific about the Institute's overall philosophy and organization. He noted that the Institute intended "to combine the work of investigation and philanthropy" in the fields of abnormal and supernormal psychology," that is, in psychopathology and psychical research (Hyslop, 1907a). Hyslop felt that the two fields "require to be studied together and treated separately under the same general supervision, partly for tactical and partly for scientific reasons" (Hyslop, 1907, p.25). It might be surmised what he meant: that it would be easier to raise funds for a clinic ("Section A") than for a psychical research group ("Section B"), while, if the abnormal and the supernormal utilize similar mechanisms, the presence of a clinic's potential research population would foster and accelerate any psychical research program.

The psychopathology clinic, under Hyslop's plan, would investigate cases of "functional mental disorder, and all psychological disturbances due even to organic troubles; functional insanity and hallucinations; amnesia or loss of memory, especially of that type often taken for serious insanity but curable by other than ordinary methods; secondary personality or unconscious mental action simulative of other agencies other than the normal consciousness; functional melancholia and vicarious or sympathetic mental aberrations; neurasthenia and psyasthenia (sic); hysteria and hysteron-epilepsy; obsessions; fixed ideas or monomanias; phobias; delusions, alcoholism, and all functional troubles that may ultimately be made to yield to the various forms of suggestion".

As if handling all this would not be enough, Hyslop added that the clinic would also investigate "the phenomena and capabilities of hypnotism ..." (Hyslop, 1907a, p.17). His attempts, however, to secure prominent psychologists and neurologists as trustees of the clinic was overwhelmingly unsuccessful.

Six years later Hyslop would launch another effort toward organizing and financing the clinic, but in 1907 his energies and enthusiasms were channeled [page 166 in the original:] toward investigation of a specific case, the so-called "Thompson-Clifford case," which first raised the question in Hyslop's mind of a specific relationship between "spirit obsession," as known to psychical researchers, and "paranoia," as known to psychopathologists. In brief, Frederic Thompson, a goldsmith, suddenly developed, in 1905, a compulsion to paint and sketch; moreover, it turned out not only that this compulsion surfaced at about the time of artist Robert Swain Gifford's death, but that Thompson's landscape paintings reflected, tree by tree, Gifford's actual outdoor environment, which Thompson never had seen. Hyslop worked with Thompson from 1907 to 1908, taking him anonymously to various mediums for sittings, and finally established that a spirit, and artist "RSG," was indeed trying to communicate through Thompson (Hyslop, 1919, p.386). The point to note is that the spirit apparently managed to influence both the patient, Thompson, and the medium, thus negating the possibility that the condition was a psychopathological one necessarily unique to the patient. By method of "cross reference," as Hyslop called it, through a medium, the fact of "spirit obsession" was established. Such a diagnosis by spiritist means obviously suggested treatment by a similar route, e.g., communication with the wayward spirit and persuasion of him or her toward some more benign activity.

While in 1905 Hyslop had suggested that mediums might, of necessity, be in an "abnormal mental condition," in 1908 he hypothesized conversely that "the communicating spirit at the time of communicating (not necessarily in his normal state in the spirit world), is in a sort of abnormal mental state, perhaps resembling our dream life or somnanbulic conditions" (Hyslop, 1908, p.188). As long as the medium did no harm but served a purpose, the abnormal condition need not be treated. Communicating spirits, however, frequently did do harm, and Hyslop drew the obvious conclusion that some means must be found to treat the abnormal conditions of mischievous discarnate souls.

Sometime around 1910, possible as late as 1912 or 1913, Hyslop systematized his method of "spiritual healing". First he would use the method of "cross reference" through the medium, described above, to establish "spirit obsession" of the patient (Hyslop, 1919, p.387). Then attention shifted from the patient to the discarnate spirit. As one of Hyslop's colleagues explained, the "object of the treatment … is to remove the obsessing personality and to educate him to the point where he realizes the harm and mischief he is doing". The aim of the therapy, while "partly to relieve the patient," was also "partly to benefit the discarnate spirit, to make him understand that he has passed through death, that he should find satisfaction in the spirit world and not trouble those who are living in this world" (Worcester and McComb, 1931, p.95).

Two articles by Hyslop, published in 1913, were long on theory but short on description in regard to his healing methods. He did specify that the diagnosis and treatment of his cases was carried out via "automatic writing" by "Dr. B's wife," most likely his neighbor across the street, Mrs. Titus Bull. He did [page 167 in the original:] laconically note one case to be of "alcoholic psychosis," and another of "sexual hallucinations". These details and whether these cases were indeed of "discarnate obsession" were "not the important thing," for, as Hyslop noted, "what we are concerned with is … that we were able to find, by mediumistic experiment, the existence of things which the psychiatrist would not have found and the cure of a case which the psychiatrist had abandoned, and this by ethical and spiritual rather than medical methods" (Hyslop, 1913c, pp.645-646). No doubt this final comment rationalized why some psychotics still did not recover.

A third article in 1913 went farther speculatively than Hyslop ever dared again. He spoke of "spiritual healing" as the "intervention of discarnate spirits in behalf of therapeutic effects" – in both mental and physical disorders (Hyslop, 1913a, 584). "Now suppose," he suggested, "that a living soul has become unable to produce the antitoxins by its own initiative." "Now if a discarnate soul should be able to get into the body or near enough to it to supply that activity it might restore the individual to his normal condition" (p.571). Hyslop recognized, however, that "the belief in spirits is more than materialism can tolerate, tho it will tolerate appeals to the utterly unintelligible (e.g. "suggestion") to escape the admission of spiritual agencies" (p.608).

After this spate of articles, Hyslop published an unsigned editorial soliciting a "Fund for Therapeutics". "We have no means," he lamented, "for carrying on that (therapeutic) work at all, tho we could have hundreds of patients if we had the means' (Hyslop, 1914, p.25). He noted that he had to turn his own house "into a sort of hospital," and, indeed, at least two well-known patients are known to have lived with the family for some time. Hyslop envisioned a "sanatorium with an equipment for making records," and estimated that an initial endowment of $250,000 would be necessary (p.26). At the time of Hyslop's death, six years later, over $180,000 had been raised (Nicol, 1973).

The lack of funds and a proper clinic didn't deter Hyslop from his theorizing and occasional healing activities. Apparently he "treated" at least eight cases, while one colleague took on ten more, and another colleague at least two; these minimum numbers are deduced from published reports of cases approached by Hyslop's technique. As the years went by, Hyslop became more confident, even haughty, and by 1918 opened boasted of his cures: "I have myself cured a man who was regarded as insane … because he could talk of nothing else than rats in his brain … . I took the man, used hypnotic suggestion and cured completely in three days." "I aided in the cure of another case diagnosed as insane … and sent to Blackwell's Island" (Hyslop, 1918, p.87). "I had come across three other cases which would or had already been diagnosed … as paranoia or hysteria, and I should have myself given the same explanation of the fact, had it not occurred to me that the method of 'cross reference' might bring out some facts which would throw light upon the perplexities of dissociation and multiple personality" (p.296). He described three cases in which what "appeared to be merely secondary personality on its [page 168 in the original:] own credentials proved, by cross reference ('through a psychic') to have come from foreign inspiration" (p.297).

Apparently it was the well-known "Doris case" that confirmed Hyslop's suspicions about "spirit obsession". Doris had been treated by one of his colleagues between 1911 and April 1914 (Prince, 1926). Most remarkably, the spiritual "communicators" in this case took it upon themselves to instruct the earthly investigators in the proper healing technique. The "controls" took up the task of showing ... that the case was (1) an instance in which an organized band of evil influences was trying to determine the girl's life for evil, and (2) that the conditions manifested in this instance were only an illustration of what was going on in thousands of cases which were treated as insane, but were perfectly curable ..." (Hyslop, 1918, p.302). The "controls" "outlined the method of treating such cases, which was to thwart the purposes of the evil 'spirit' in any special instance, to extort confession of their deeds, and then to remove them from contact with the living victim" (p.308). He elsewhere added that it was "not necessary to suppose that these invasions ("by foreign and discarnate agencies") were the primary cause of the trouble. Organic lesions sometimes open the way ..." (Hyslop, 1919, p.387). In any case he considered it "high time to prosecute experiments on a large scale ..." (p.400).

Hyslop never fully realized his aim, but colleagues did, or at least tried. Upon his death in 1920, the American Institute for Scientific Research dissolved, with "Section A," the psychopathology clinic, still uninaugurated. "Section B," the American Society for Psychical Research, emancipated itself, but soon faced, in 1925, an amalgam of Hyslop's former colleagues who, through founding the Boston Society for Psychical Research, hoped both to reabsorb the American Society and reestablish

Hyslop's point of view (Worcester, 1926). The same group of colleagues chartered, in 1927, the "James H. Hyslop Foundation, Inc.," headquartered in New York City, "to aid physicians in the study of physic (sic) phenomena in relation to mental and physical illness" (Hyslop Foundation, 1927).

The reports of the Hyslop Foundation were quite curious, to say the least. The physician who worked with Hyslop from the beginning, Dr. Titus Bull, served as president of the foundation and apparently as chief investigator/ clinician also. As before, there were plans, rather hopes, to establish "a center where patients may be under the constant care of nurses and treated by competent physicians who will report, in scientific publications, the results of the treatment and the analyses of cases" (Hyslop Foundation, 1929). The call was, once again, for a $250,000 initial endowment, of which over $150,000 was received by 1934. One new element, unanticipated by Hyslop, was provision for salaried psychics specifically trained for this investigative/ therapeutic work. Another innovation, of perhaps debatable merit, was the use of various quasi-scientific euphemisms, such as "lucidity" for "psychic abilities," and [page 169 in the original:] "developed psychic instrument" for "medium". After 1934 there were no signs of continued activity by the James H. Hyslop Foundation.

What conclusion can be drawn? In a previous article, "The 'Subliminal' versus the 'Subconscious' ...," I suggested that American physicians and laymen found the psychical research concept of the "subliminal" of greater aesthetic and heuristic value than the academic psychologic concept of the "subconscious" (Powell, 1979). The concept of the subliminal explained more phenomena more economically, across normal, abnormal, and "supernormal" psychology. The psychical research notion thus seemed more scientific than its more academic competitor. While the case is not as clear-cut for Hyslop's concept of "spirit obsession," as invasion of a patient's mind by a mischievous discarnate soul, the alternative, primarily neuroanatomic, explanations of paranoia were not necessarily more scientific. Just as acceptance of a dynamic subliminal provided a rationale for psychotherapy, while the notion of a static subconscious did not, so, too, acceptance of the possibility of "spirit obsession" implied a specific treatment approach toward patients who otherwise would be considered beyond hope. Hyslop's brand of "spiritism," or "psychical research," reflected an early twentieth century bias toward scientific hypotheses that provided for the continuity and evolution of phenomena and were thus elegantly comprehensive in their explanatory power. A spiritist view placed obsession/ paranoia, the abnormal, in the context of normal phenomena, while a neuroanatomical view did not. [page 170 in the original:]

#

Notes

(Boston Society for Psychical Research), "Boston Psychic Seceders Hope to Absorb Parent Body: Dr. Worcester Presides Over Meeting at the Vendome, Attended by 100 Persons – Dr. Prince's Offer Criticized," Boston Herald, 10 March 1925. Item #1454, vertical file, American Society for Psychical Research library.

Bull, T., "Why 'Mental and Moral Mastery Aids Physical Health," J Am Soc Psychical Res 7:659-663, 1913.

Bull, T., An Analysis of Unusual Experiences in Healing Relative to Diseased Minds and Results of Materialism Foreshadowed. New York: James H. Hyslop Foundation, 1932.

Bull, T., Nature, Man, and Destiny. New York: James H. Hyslop Foundation, 1933.

Bull, T., Man's Great Adventure. New York: James H. Hyslop Foundation, 1934.

Hyslop, B., Interviews with the Author, 21 January and 1 February 1973.

Hyslop. G., "James H. Hyslop: His Contributions to Psychical Research," J Am Soc Psychical Res 44:129-137, 1950.

Hyslop, J.H., "Autobiography. 6 March 1904 and 6 August 1916," Manuscript in the possession of Beatrice Hyslop, Jackson Heights, New York. Copy in American Society for Psychical Research library.

Hyslop, J.H., "Letter to Weston D. Bayley, 17 January 1905," quoted in Bayley, Weston D., "Entrance upon Psychical Research and Characteristics" (re Hyslop), J Am Soc Psychical Res 14:433-440, 1920.

Hyslop, J.H., Problems of Philosophy or Principles of Epistemology and Metaphysics. Boston: Small, Maynard & Co., 1905b.

Hyslop, J.H., Science and a Future Life. Boston: Herbert B. Turner & Co., 1905c.

Hyslop, J.H., "An Important Object of the Society Will Be to Expose Charlatans as Well as to Collect Well Authenticated Evidence of Psychic Manifestations – The Subject Always Fascinating," New York Times, 24 June 1906a.

Hyslop, J.H., Enigmas of Psychical Research. London: G.P. Putnam & Sons, 1906b.

Hyslop, J.H., Borderlands of Psychical Research. Boston: Herbert B. Turner & Co., 1906c.

Hyslop, J.H., "Objects of the Institute" (re American Institute for Scientific Research), J Am Soc Psychical Res 1:15-28. 1907d.

Hyslop, J.H., "Prospectus of the American Institute for Scientific Research," Proc Am Soc Psychical Res 1:23-72, 1907b.

Hyslop, J.H., Psychical Research and the Resurrection. Boston: Small, Maynard & Co., 1908.

Hyslop, J.H., "The Abnormal and the Supernormal," J Am Soc Psychical Res 4:375-378, 1910.

Hyslop, J.H., "Spiritual Healing," J Am Soc Psychical Res 7:577-610, 1913a.

Hyslop, J.H., "A Neglected Type," J Am Soc Psychical Res 7:611-634, 1913b.

Hyslop, J.H., "A Case of Alcoholism," J Am Soc Psychical Res 7:635-647, 1913c.

Hyslop, J.H., Psychical Research and Survival. London: G. Bell & Sons, Ltd., 1913d.

Hyslop, J.H., "Fund for Therapeutics," J Am Soc Psychical Res 8:25-26, 1914.

Hyslop, J.H., <u>Life after Death: Problems of the Future Life and Its Nature</u>. New York: E.P. Dutton & Co., 1918.

Hyslop, J.H., <u>Contact with the Other World: The Latest Evidence as to Communication with the Dead</u>. New York: The Century Co., 1919.

(Hyslop Foundation), "Organize to Push Psysic [sic] Studies: Sponsors of Hyslop Foundation to Perpetuate Memory of Columbia Professor," New York Times, 27 October 1927.

(Hyslop Foundation), "Report to the Annual Meeting of James H. Hyslop Foundation, Inc." separate reports dated October 1927, October 1928, October 1931, and October 1933, in the possession of Beatice Hyslop, Jackson Heights, New York.

Nicol, F., Interview with the Author, 16 April 1973.

Powell, R.C., "The 'Subliminal' versus the 'Subconscious' in the American Acceptance of Psychoanalysis, 1906-1910," J Hist Behav Sci 15:155-165, 1979.

Prince, W.F., "James Hervey Hyslop: Biographical Sketch and Impressions," J Am Soc Psychical Res 14:425-432, 1920.

Prince, W.F., <u>The Psychic in the House</u>. Boston: Boston Society for Psychical Research, 1926.

Prince, W.F., "Two Cures of Paranoia by Experimental Appeals to Purported Obsessing Spirits," Boston Soc Psychical Res Bulletin 6:36-71, 1927. [page 171 in the original:]

Worcester, E., "Presidential Address," in <u>Addresses by Drs. Worcester and McDougall – Document III</u>. Boston: Boston Society for Psychical Research, 1926.

Worcester, E., <u>Life's Adventure: The Story of a Varied Career.</u> New York: Charles Scribner's Sons, 1932.

Worcester, E., <u>Making Life Better: An Application of Religion and Psychology to Human Problems</u>. New York: Charles Scribner's Sons, 1933.

Worcester, E. & McComb, S., <u>Body, Mind, and Spirit</u>. Boston: Marshall Jones & Co., 1931.

#

&&&

The Author's Comments in 2015:

This research originally was presented before the Illinois Psychiatric Society annual meeting, Rosemont, IL, November 1980.

This article originally was published in Wallace, Edwin R, and. Pressley, Lucius C., eds. <u>Essays in the History of Psychiatry</u>, A Tenth Anniversary Supplementary Volume to the Psychiatric Forum 161-171, 1980.

The opening abstract was not part of the original manuscript.

The original starting place of each page of text is indicated, so that previous citations of this article still will be accurate.

At the time this manuscript was accepted, Dr. Powell was a "self-supported scholar" practicing psychiatry in the northwest suburbs of Chicago.

While the original text did not underscore book titles or place article titles in quotes, both are done here. Whenever a few quoted words fall at the end of a sentence, the period has been placed outside of the quotation mark rather than inside, as had been done in the original text. In the endnotes, colons after authors' names have been replaced with commas. The following other minor changes have been made to the text: p.161: "a membership of 1200" has been replaced by "a membership of 1,200"; "p.162, "Hyslop, G, 1950" has been replaced with "Hyslop, G., 1950"; "scepticism" [British spelling] has been replaced with "skepticism"

[American spelling]; p.163, "scepticism" has been replaced with "skepticism"; p.164: "Hyslop argued that while the phenomena" has been replaced with "Hyslop argued that the phenomena"; p.165: "under Hyslop's plan would investigate" has been replaced with "under Hyslop's plan, would investigate"; p.166: "Thompson had never seen" has been replaced with "Thompson never had seen"; ", e.g. communication" had been replaced with ", e.g., communication"; "Mr. Titus Bull" has been replaced with "Mrs. Titus Bull" [Eva McComb Bull (1872-1954), wife of neurologist Titus Bull, MD (1871-1949)]; p.167: "another of" has been replaced with "and another of"; "in behalf of" has NOT been replaced by "on behalf of" as this indeed was the phrasing used by Hyslop and his contemporaries; "Nichol, 1973" has been replaced with "Nicol, 1973" – as this is a reference to J. Fraser Nicol, a prominent psychical researcher who died in 1989; p.168: "("through a psychic")" has been replaced with "('through a psychic')"; p.169: "mischievous discarnate/ soul" has been replaced with "mischievous discarnate soul"; "would otherwise be considered" has been replaced with "otherwise would be considered"; p.170: "References" has been replaced with "Notes"; "Relatives to Diseased" has been replaced with "Relative to Diseased"; "Nichol, F." has been replaced with "Nicol, F."; "The Subliminal versus the Subconscious in" has been replaced with "The 'Subliminal' versus the 'Subconscious' in".

Extra Endnotes

As indicated (somewhat cryptically) in the original endnotes, I interviewed Hyslop's third child and youngest of two daughters – Beatrice Fry Hyslop (1899-1973) in New York City on January 21 and February 1, 1973. She died July 23, 1973 – so, once again, luck was on my side as I pursued my research. Most likely the materials then in her possession concerning her father went to the American Society for Psychical Research, whose offices remain at 5 West 73rd Street in New York City.

Myers, Frederic W. H., "The Subliminal Consciousness:

Chapter VI: The Mechanism of Hysteria," Proceedings of the Society for Psychical Research 1893; 9:3-25; pp.7, 12-13, 15; cited by many authors as a main point of introduction of Sigmund Freud's work to the English-speaking public; now available on the internet via Google Books.

Freud, Sigmund, "Psychoanalysis and Telepathy," presented in 1922 but not published until 1941 and not re-published in English translation until 1943; new and annotated translation in The Standard Edition of the Complete Psychological Works of Sigmund Freud, 1955;18:173-194. Intriguingly, Freud's principal translator in The Standard Edition, James Strachey, is said to have been originally led to Freud's work by a footnote in a book by psychical researcher Frederic W. H. Myers; see, Meisel, Perry & Kendrick, Walter M., eds., Bloomsbury/ Freud : the letters of James and Alix Strachey, 1924-1925. New York: Basic Books, 1986, pp.26-27.

Since the first appearance of this article, the following relevant studies have been published:
Matlock, James G., "Leonora or Leonore? A Note on Mrs. Piper's First Name," The Journal of the American Society for Psychical Research. July 1988; 82:281-290; makes it clear that the first name was "Leonora" not "Leonore".   http://jamesgmatlock.net/wp-content/uploads/2014/02/Matlock-1988-Leonora.pdf
Aziz, Robert, C. G. Jung's Psychology of Religion and Synchronicity. Albany: State University of New York Press, 1990; see especially pp.99-102. Aziz notes, among other things, that Sigmund Freud had been a corresponding member of the Society for Psychical Research in London since 1911 and an honorary fellow of the American Society for Psychical Research since 1915.
Charet, F. X., Spiritualism and the Foundations of C. G. Jung's Psychology. Albany: State University of New York Press, 1993; see especially pp.42-43 re Sigmund Freud's clarification in 1912 for psychical researchers of the notion of "multiple personality".
Phillips, Adam, Terrors and Experts. Cambridge, MA:

Harvard University Press, 1995; see especially pp.21-22 re "thought transference" ("telepathy") in the psychoanalytic session, as discussed by Sigmund Freud and Sandor Ferenczi.

Azaunce, Miriam, "Is it schizophrenia or spirit possession?" J Social Distress Homeless. July 1995; 4(3):255-263.

Hinshelwood, Robert D., "Psychoanalysis in Britain: Points of Cultural Access, 1893-1918," pp.239- 292, in Altounian, J.; Fonagy, P.; Gabbard, G.O.; Grotstein, J.S.; Hinshelwood, R.D.; Jimenez, J.P.; Kernberg, O.F.; Leo, G.; and, Resnik, S., Psychoanalysis and Its Borders. Lecce, Italy: Frenis Zero Press, 2012; see especially p.247: "He [psychical researcher Frederic W. H. Myers] picked out an image of Freud as one who had contacted the 'other world' through the unconscious life of hysterical patients."

Sommer, Andreas, "Psychical research and the origins of American psychology: Hugo Münsterberg, William James, and Eusapia Palladino," Hist Human Sci. Apr 2012; 25(2): 23–44. http://www.ncbi.nlm.nih.gov/pmc/articles/PMC3552602/

Irmak, M. Kemal, "Schizophrenia or possession?" J Relig Health. 2014 Jun; 53(3):773-777. [This article created quite a stir in the clinical and academic communities when it appeared in print; that being said, a coherent rebuttal has not yet been found. A search of the world's medical literature at PubMed.gov reveals that there is an extensive clinical literature on "spirit possession". The issue seems significant enough to justify including this article's abstract here: "Schizophrenia is typically a life-long condition characterized by acute symptom exacerbations and widely varying degrees of functional disability. Some of its symptoms, such as delusions and hallucinations, produce great subjective psychological pain. The most common delusion types are as follows: 'My feelings and movements are controlled by others in a certain way' and 'They put thoughts in my head that are not mine'. Hallucinatory experiences are generally voices talking to the patient or among themselves. Hallucinations are a cardinal positive symptom of schizophrenia which deserves careful study in the hope it will give information about the pathophysiology of the disorder. We thought that many so-called hallucinations in schizophrenia are really illusions related to a real environmental stimulus. One approach to this hallucination problem is to consider the possibility of a demonic world. Demons are unseen creatures that are believed to exist in all major religions and have the power to possess humans and control their body. Demonic possession can manifest with a range of bizarre behaviors which could be interpreted as a number of different psychotic disorders with delusions and hallucinations. The hallucination in schizophrenia may therefore be an illusion – a false interpretation of a real sensory image formed by demons. A local faith healer in our region helps the patients with schizophrenia. His method of treatment seems to be successful because his patients become symptom free after 3 months. Therefore, it would be useful for medical professions to work together with faith healers to define better treatment pathways for schizophrenia."

#

PART TWO

The "Subliminal" versus the "Subconscious" in the American Acceptance of Psychoanalysis, 1906-1910.

[page 155 in the original:] *Insofar as Frederic W.H. Myers' conceptions of the "subliminal" were spread by the Boston-based "Emmanuel movement" for medically supervised religious psychotherapy (fl.1906-1910), the movement probably did more to help than to hinder American acceptance of Freudian ideas. Certainly, many academic psychologists' conceptions of the "unconscious" and "subconscious" were a hindrance.*

Nathan Hale's Freud and the Americans concludes that the Boston–based "Emmanuel movement" for medically supervised religious psychotherapy, most active from 1906 to about 1910, helped "prepare the way for psychoanalysis," but also helped compromise American acceptance of psychoanalytic ideas. For the cause of this second effect Hale singles out the movement's "enthusiasm for the mysterious subliminal self".[1]

Without doubt this uniquely "medico-religious" healing movement, led by the Rev. Drs. Elwood Worcester (1862-1940) and Samuel McComb (1864-1938), played an important role in the dissemination of psychotherapeutic conceptions among the American public, ultimately arousing the ire, concern, and interest of the American medical profession – all on the eve of Sigmund Freud's visit to the United States in September 1909.[2] While basically agreeing with Hale's conclusions – with his first more than his second – and while recognizing these conclusions as minor in the context of his broader study, I believe we would do well to explore further the concept of the "subliminal/ subconscious," its relations to Freud's theories, and its place in the lives and writings of the Emmanuel movement's founders.[3] Picking up where Hale's intriguing comments leave off, I wish to address the question of how theories promulgated by the Emmanuel movement compared with those held by contemporary laymen, psychologists, physicians, and clergymen. To be more specific, exactly how did the Emmanuel movement "prepare the way for psychoanalysis" and what role did the concept of the "subliminal" play in this story?

To begin with, there is the matter of timing. Although after 1910 academic psychologists flooded the market with refutations of the subliminal/ unconscious, in 1908-1909, when the Emmanuel movement was at its height, most easily available considerations of the topic either supported the Emmanuel view or failed to argue clearly for an alternative. Among the era's most widely read books were William James' Varieties of Religious Experience ... (1902), Frederic W. H. Myers' Human Personality ... (1903), and [page 156 in the original:] J. Milne Bramwell's Hypnotism ... (1903), all of which contained sizable, provocative discussions of the subliminal/ unconscious. In contrast, most reviewers found The Subconscious (1906) by psychologist Joseph Jastrow virtually unreadable.[4] Laymen {/laywomen} who did read Jastrow tended to interpret his sanction in terms of notions they had learned elsewhere, as, for example, from turn-of-the-century popularizers of the subliminal such as Thomas Jay Hudson and Alfred T. Schofield. Two other psychologists, Boris Sidis and Morton Prince, dazzled the public with their descriptions of "multiple personality" in 1905 and 1906, but neither yet argued a view distinctly incompatible with laymen's {/laywomen's} views of the subliminal/ unconscious. If anything, the works of psychologists Jastrow, Sidis, and Prince seemed notably shallow and dry next to the earlier, still popular, tradition of James, Myers, and Bramwell, a tradition in which Religion and Medicine ... (1908), the Emmanuel "handbook," found its place.

Despite his popularity, academic psychologists have remained eternally ambivalent toward William James (1842-1910), for he found insufferable, if not humorous, his colleagues' pretentions toward scientific rigor as they ignored a multiplicity of human phenomena. Certainly not every psychologist would have agreed when James dated the dawn of modern psychology to 1886, the year of the discovery that "there is not only the consciousness of the ordinary field, ... but an addition thereto in the shape of a set of memories, thoughts, and feelings which are extra-marginal,"[5] and probably not every psychologist caught the significance of the date. In 1886 the London Society for Psychical Research, of which James was a member and later president, published the massive, detailed, and critical Phantasms of the Living, a study of telepathically communicated veridical hallucinations, to the end of which was appended a long note by Frederic W. H. Myers (1843-1901).[6] This cautious, speculative, widely read note, to which James no doubt refers, presaged Myer's later onslaught of articles developing a unitary, psychological theory of hysteria, hypnosis, telepathy, genius, and the *vis medicatrix naturae* – that is, the theory of the "subliminal self".[7]

Myers proposed to expand the Hebartian, Fechnerian concept of the "subliminal," a term meaning "beneath the threshold" and already used to describe "those sensations which are too feeble to be individually recognized," into a broader, more comprehensive concept that would include "all that takes place beneath the ordinary margin of consciousness".[8] Thus Myers' subliminal comprised *normal* organic functions plus elaborative mental processes not recognizable through introspection, *abnormal* "disaggregations of personality as seen in hysteria and due to excessive permeability of the psychical threshold," and *supernormal* phenomena such as telepathy and communication with departed souls. Somewhat analogous with Carl Jung's later defined "racial unconsciousness," Myers' subliminal described a domain far more vast and profound than the normal "supraliminal" consciousness: "no Self of which we can here have cognizance is in reality more than a fragment of a larger Self – revealed in a fashion at once shifting and limited through an organism not so framed as to afford it full manifestation".[9] Elsewhere,

Myers suggested that "our habitual or empirical consciousness may consist of a mere selection from a multitude of thoughts and sensations, of which some at least are equally conscious with those that we empirically know".[10]

British neurologist J. Milne Bramwell (1852-1925) granted that "the subliminal consciousness theory does not satisfactorily explain all the problems of hypnosis," but felt "at all events indebted to it for a clearer conception not only of the condition as a whole, but also of many of its component parts".[11] Just as Myers defined hysteria as "an undue permeability of the psychical diaphragm which separates ordinary consciousness from [page 157 in the original:] the depths below," he defined hypnotism as to "purposely increase the permeability of the psychical diaphragm in such a way as to push down beneath it various forms of pain and annoyance which we are anxious to get rid of from our waking consciousness".[12] Disregarding, as most clinicians did, Myers' concern with the supernormal, Bramwell considered the subliminal theory to have the merit of accommodating most of the then-known phenomena of normal and abnormal behavior, while suggesting a mechanism for these behaviors and providing a rationale for the use of psychotherapy.

Though Myers' theory may seem excessively spiritual, one must consider the alternative existing at the time. Bramwell suggested that "instead of attempting to explain hypnosis by the arrested action of some of the brain centers which subserve normal life," the subliminal theory would, rather, postulate the arousal of "certain powers over which we normally have no control".[13] That is, Myers would "explain the phenomena of hypnotism by the intelligent and voluntary action of a secondary or subliminal consciousness".[14] Thus, unlike the static, neurologic theories of "unconscious cerebration," Myers' was dynamic, postulating motivated psychological processes quite different from those of normal consciousness but conceptually adequate to explain normal as well as abnormal phenomena.

Though James, Myers, and Bramwell – philosopher, essayist, and physician – felt the necessity of understanding "extramarginal" phenomena, most academic psychologists did not. There are several reasons for this. First, most psychologists, confining themselves to a study of the mind, identified mind with consciousness; thus to the extent a phenomenon were un-conscious it would be considered un-psychological and consigned to the physiologist. For example, James M. Baldwin (1861-1934) complained of the "inherent contradiction in terms of the expression "unconscious mental activity,"[15] while Edward B. Titchener (1867-1927) first defined "subconsciousness ... as an extension of the consciousness beyond the limits of observation," then deduced that "the subconsciousness is not a part of the subject matter of psychology".[16]

A second reason why most academic psychologists showed little interest in extramarginal phenomena is that most felt they had adequately demonstrated both (a) "marginal attention" as continuous with and in no way essentially different from normal consciousness, and (b) "subliminal sensation" as purely physiological without cognitive or affective components. For example, James R. Angell (1869-1949) spoke of the subconscious as "a dimmer region of partial consciousness" and of the unconscious as "those marginal neural actions which evidently modify the reactions we make, without, however, producing notable mental changes".[17]

Third, psychologists considered therapy (beyond training or education) as the province of physicians – or quacks; insofar as they prided themselves on being scientists, most psychologists saw no reason to be concerned with hypnotism or hysteria. This disdainful attitude is demonstrated by one of Titchener's comments when, after demolishing the concept of the subconscious, he then allows that "science cannot ask the physician to give up a theory that works".[18] Philosophers, essayists, and physicians might feel a need for understanding extramarginal phenomena, but most academic psychologists did not.

Notable exceptions to the rule on therapy were Pierre Janet (1859-1947), who first earned a degree in psychology, then in medicine; Morton Prince (1854-1929), a neurologist who devoted his life to psychology; and Boris Sidis (1867-1923), a follower of Janet, a student of James and Prince, who also moved from psychology into medicine. Each concerned himself with the practical, therapeutic aspects of studying extramarginal [page 158 in the original:] phenomena, though not without reflecting the other preconceptions of academic psychology. Revealingly, Janet disdained the terms "subconscious" and "unconscious," preferring instead to speak of "secondary consciousness,"[19] while Prince favored "co-consciousness,"[20] and Sidis "sub-waking consciousness".[21] Each considered the extramarginal phenomena of hysteria, such as dual personality and the dissociation of affects from ideas, as essentially akin to normal consciousness, which they identified with mind.

In sharp contrast to Myers and Bramwell, who envisioned in hysteria strong "subliminal tendencies" bursting through the "psychical diaphragm," Janet characterized hysteria as a type of weakness and exhaustion leading to the disintegration of consciousness and the "migration of certain psychological phenomena into a special group," a secondary consciousness.[22] Prince and Sidis agreed. Accordingly, when Janet did use the term "subconsciousness," he defined it as an "exaggerated absent-mindedness" distinctly peculiar to hysteria,[23] a point on which Prince would agree[24] but Sidis would hesitate; Sidis felt these phenomena were sometimes seen in normal.[25]

Janet and Sidis most emphatically, Prince less emphatically, challenged Myers' assertion that the subliminal exercised a control over the organism both "more potent and profound" than that of normal consciousness, and exercised "neither blindly nor wisely but with intelligent caprice".[26] "The poor patients whom I studied," scoffed Janet, "had no genius; the phenomena which had become subconscious with them were very simple phenomena such as among other men are a part of their personal consciousness and excite no wonder".[27] When Sidis declared in italics that "Morbid mental states have no meaning,"[28] he was attempting to outshout not only nascent Freudians but also any followers of Myers who would impute intelligence to anything but the waking consciousness. On this issue Prince had to equivocate; while denying that there is normally any distinct subconscious self, he recognized the difficulty of deciding which of several "co-conscious" selves should be granted superiority and control.[29]

Thus, academic psychologists and Myers failed to see "eye to eye". What about Sigmund Freud (1856-1939) and Myers? Freud's biographer, Ernest Jones (1879-1958) notes that Myers was the first to give an account in English of Freud and Josef Breurer's work,[30] and that Jones himself first sampled Freud's work through two case histories reprinted by Myers in Human Personality and Its Survival of Bodily Death (1903).[31] Nevertheless, in the midst of the pro- and antipsychoanalytic polemics surrounding World War One, Jones found it convenient to link Myers to Jung, the recently disposed colleague, and then to draw a disparaging view of Myers' work. Myers' conception of the unconscious, commented Jones, "might well be called the 'limbo conception,' for in it the unconscious is regarded as an obscure region of the mind, the content of which is largely characterized by neglect and oblivion". "According to this view," Jones went on, "the unconscious part of the mind is a sort of lumber-room to which various mental processes get relegated when they are in a state of inactivity. These processes are then usually considered to be of only quite secondary importance in comparison with conscious ones, and they are accorded no initiative of their own, or any primary dynamic functions, being purely of a passive nature."[32] Apparently Jones amalgamated and confused Myers' writings with those of the academic psychologists, for it is the latters' work that Jones describes.

One of Freud's most important theoretical papers, "A Note on the Unconscious in Psycho-Analysis" (1912), published in Myers' home journal, the Proceedings of the (London) Society for Psychical Research,[33] extended the concept of a threshold and the [page 159 in the original:] concept of dynamic mental processes that both Myers and Freud had borrowed from Herbart and Fechner.[34] Seemingly in agreement with

Myers, against Janet, Freud argued that certain ideas remain unconscious not through any weakness but through an inherent difference in nature. "The term *unconscious*," wrote Freud, "... designates not only latent ideas in general [the preconscious], but especially ideas with a certain dynamic character, ideas apart from consciousness in spite of their intensity and activity [the unconscious proper]."[35] Freud and Myers both found consciousness nonsynonymous with mind and incomparable with the unconscious, which operates through rules of its own. However, whereas Myers suggested that the human organism is "not so framed as to afford ... full manifestation" to the unconscious, Freud phrased his similar conclusion in terms of the unconscious ideas themselves. Furthermore, Freud, more clearly than Myers, recognized *two* thresholds: a more flexible one between the conscious and the preconscious, and a more rigid one, governed by the dynamics of repression, between the preconscious and the unconscious proper.

Freud, in The Interpretation of Dreams (1900), foreshadowing numerous later passages in which he berated psychologists for their insistence that consciousness is the essence of mind,[36] cited his agreement with psychologist Theodor Lipps – and, I would add, his implicit agreement with Myers – that "the unconscious must be assumed to be the general basis of psychical life". "The unconscious," Freud continued, "is the larger sphere, which includes within it the smaller sphere of the conscious. Everything conscious has an unconscious preliminary stage; whereas what is unconscious may remain at that stage and nevertheless claim to be regarded as having the full value of a psychical process. The unconscious is the true psychical reality."[37] While this view was not confined to Freud, Lipps, and Myers, the point is that it was vehemently denounced, as noted above, by academic psychologists, at a time when it was held widely by the public.

The contrast between laymen's {/laywomen's} and psychologists' views of the subconscious can be seen clearly in a comparison of two articles that appeared near the peak of the Emmanuel controversy: Prince's introduction to a symposium on "subconscious phenomena" (1910), featuring contributions by six eminent psychologists; and a rather "Freudian" article on dream imagery that appeared in the Proceedings of the American Society for Psychical Research (1909). Prince distinguished six meanings of the subconscious, only two of which he considered seriously: "dissociated or split-off ideas" and "pure neural processes unaccompanied by any mentation whatsoever".[38] The lay article distinguished "three typical uses" of the term "subconscious": the phenomena of marginal consciousness; the phenomena of multiple personality; and "forms of mentation that are never 'in' consciousness at all, that are never (in ordinary experience) conscious; yet which must be assumed in order to make what is conscious intelligible". " 'Subconsciousness,' in this sense," the author contended, "means that 'mind' is not co-extensive with 'consciousness' but includes along with conscious mentation states and processes of which the conscious self is only indirectly aware." "It is the third use of 'subconscious'," he continued, "which suffers from a criticism on the part of psychologists ..., and it is this use that is finding a permanent lodgment in literary English."[39] Without mentioning Freud, the author attributes this usage to Myers, and then goes on to contrast Myers' view with Janet's.

In summary, though empirically derived, Myers' conceptions, unlike Freud's, did not lead to empirically tested and revised concepts. My stance, however, is with James, who felt that while others "did work far more objective," and while "Myers' belief in the ubiquity and great extent of the Subliminal will demand a far larger number of facts than [page 160 in the original:] sufficed to persuade him before the next generation of psychologists shall become persuaded," Myers "nevertheless will stand as the original announcer of a theory which ... makes an epoch not only in medical but in psychological science, because it brings in an entirely new conception of our mental possibilities".[40]

Having discussed the concept of the subliminal, we now turn to the orientation and writings of Elwood Worcester and Samuel McComb, founders of the Emmanuel movement.

Despite Worcester and McComb's repeated claim that theirs was "the psychology of the schools," theirs was the psychology of James, Myers, and Bramwell – not to mention Hudson and Schofield – as most critiques of their work recognized.[41] What most critics failed to recognize and appreciate, however, was (1) the lasting effect of the dying Gustav Theodor Fechner (1801-1887) upon his pupil Worcester (see below) – an influence far more profound that than of Fechner's writings upon Freud or Myers – and (2) the deep commitment both Worcester and McComb felt toward explicating "the Gospel of a Savior's Love" and "the Religion of the Spirit and of Power" – two great principles of reconciliation and rapport that they saw clarified in the light of the subliminal concept.[42]

During a period in his youth when he still was feeling fatherless and alone in the world, Worcester met the aging Fechner while studying under Wilhelm Wundt in Leipzig. Worcester drew close to Fechner during the last months of the philosopher/ psychologist's life, and espoused his conviction that science is a question of method, not of matter, and that there just as well could be "a science of the immaterial and spiritual ... as of the physical and material".[43] Fechner found all of nature to be the outward manifestation of one psychical continuum, G-d's soul, and he judged that man's consciousness, because of its comparatively high threshold, contains only fragments of the soul of G-d, otherwise called the subliminal.[44] The famous law of stimulus thresholds, the "Fechner law" of psychophysics [(Sensation) = k log R (stimulus)], came to Fechner in a flash as he lay on his bed, a revelation that any increase in spiritual intensity would correspond to an increase in corporal movement.[45] Fechner first noted the theory in his mystical Zend Avesta (1851), a treatise on the "earth soul" paraphrased by Worcester as The Living Word (1908).[46] Thus, Worcester's grasp of the subliminal harked back to Fechner, who applied the theory of a threshold even to G-d,[47] and Worcester meant The Living Word to supplement, "from the philosophical side" (1908), the Emmanuel handbook, Religion and Medicine ... .[48]

Except for the special spiritual uses to which he put the subliminal concept, Worcester's views closely paralleled those of Myers.[49] Worcester and McComb saw the subliminal as a larger consciousness lacking definite physiologic basis, though they conceded that it might be the physical concomitant of the sympathetic nervous system.[50] They saw the subconscious as the source of power which "quickens our intellectual processes," "heightens our willpower," and "cannot be regarded as pathological"; as the source of genius, emotional upheaval, conversion, and the *vis medicatrix naturae*, a "normal part of our spiritual nature".[51]

When the Emmanuel movement came under fire in 1909, physicians most cogently discussed the validity of distinguishing "functional" from "organic" disorder – for the movement claimed to treat only the former – and the propriety of any nonmedical use of hypnosis, a practice which the leaders of the movement willingly gave up. Physicians' comments on the subliminal/ subconscious, however, generally relied on psychologist Hugo Münsterberg's dictum: "the story of the subconscious mind can be told in three [page 161 in the original:] words: there is none".[52] This quote, which repeatedly appeared in the medical press at the height of the Emmanuel controversy, reveals the pathetic level of argument most physicians were able to muster against the concept of a subliminal/ subconscious. Physicians realized this, however, and worked to improve their argument and their claim for psychotherapy as a medical prerogative.[53]

Theological discussion of the subliminal/ subconscious stood in marked contrast to the medical considerations. For example, a clergyman {/clergywoman} browsing the Hibbert Journal for January 1909 would have come upon a passable critique of the Emmanuel movement, William James on Fechner's doctrine of the earth-soul, plus two articles on psychical research.[54] Turning next to the American Journal of Theology,he {/she} would have found a first-rate article, "Religion and the Subconscious," and if he {/she} kept an eye on the latest books, George B. Cutten's Psychological Phenomena of Christianity (1909) would have offered a scholarly survey conservatively nothing that "if G-d works directly in man He {/She} must work through the subconscious".[55]

The concept of the subliminal/ subconscious was nothing new to educated clergy when the Emmanuel publications began to appear in 1908 and 1909. Two popularizers, Hudson and Schofield, had been giving the subliminal a religious interpretation since the mid-1890s, and Edwin D. Starbuck's masterful Psychology of Religion ... (1899) used "subliminal" and "subconscious" interchangeably.[56] Editors of the Hibbert Journal for 1903-1904 presented a critical, rousing debate over the "subliminal self," and already by 1905 one clergyman {/clergywoman} had asked whether, in the theological appropriation of the subliminal concept, "the errors involved cost more heavily than can be paid by the truth gained".[57] After British divine William Sanday deigned, in 1910, to make the subliminal consciousness the "locus of the Deity of the Incarnate Christ," theologians began to criticize Myers' concept.[58] But in 1908 and 1909, most voices were with James, Myers, and the subliminal/ subconscious.

From both the religious and the medical sides one could argue that the Emmanuel movement failed to follow Myers closely enough, for Myers carefully stressed that the subliminal was as yet an hypothesis, and Myers himself saw the importance of Freud's work. Nonetheless, in contrast to the academic psychologists, who asserted that the subconscious was a static, abnormal, and either neural or dissociated from consciousness seen as the essence of mind, Worcester and McComb disseminated a view of the subconscious as dynamic, normal, essentially different from and yet influencing consciousness, and as a reality far more important than the consciousness taken for granted. While they did not spread Freud's understanding of the mechanisms governing unconscious phenomena, for they were relatively unacquainted with Freud's work, the Emmanuelites did, insofar as they followed Myers, propagate conceptions essential to grasping Freud's concepts. Thus, if the Emmanuel movement can be seen as helping to "prepare the way for psychoanalysis" through prompting discussion of the issues, the movement's enthusiasm for the concept of the subliminal appears as an essential part of this process.

Using Shakow and Rapaport's differentiation between *concepts* and *conceptions*, that is, between the sharply defined terms themselves and the broader matrices from which they crystalize,[59] the various *concepts* of the subconscious held by Janet, Prince, and Sidis rarely touched upon Freud's conceptual world. I conclude with Shakow and Rapaport that thought the *conceptions* of Janet, Prince, and Sidis may have "prepared the ground for the acceptance of Freudian *conceptions* of the unconscious," they could not "prepare the ground for Freud's *concepts*".[60] While Myers no more shared Freud's [page 162 in the original:] *concept* of the unconscious than did Janet, Prince, or Sidis, my argument is that Myers' empirically derived *conceptions* were far more congenial to Freud's than eithers could have been to the preconceptions of the academic psychologists. Insofar as Myers' conceptions were spread by the Emmanuel movement, the movement probably did more to help than to hinder the acceptance of Freudian ideas. Certainly the academic psychologists' conceptions were a hindrance.

#

Notes

1. Nathan G. Hale, Jr., Freud and the Americans: The Beginnings of Psychoanalysis in the United States, 1876-1917 (New York: Oxford University Press, 1971), p.249.

2. For a more detailed discussion of the Emmanuel movement, see my dissertation, which includes the first use of the "Worcester Papers," discovered in 1973. Robert C. Powell, Healing and Wholeness: Helen Flanders Dunbar (1902-59) and an Extra-Medical Origin of the American Psychosomatic Movement, 1906-36 (Ann Arbor: ProQuest (order # AAT 7502415), chap.5.

3. The terms "unconscious," "subliminal," and "subconscious" recur throughout this manuscript with different meanings according to

different users. The following table of approximate equivalents may be helpful:

	said	*seem to have meant*
academic psychologists	unconscious	neural
	subliminal	neural
	subconscious	marginally conscious
Myers	subliminal	Freud's unconscious
Worcester and McComb	subconscious	soul, Myers' subliminal, and Freud's unconscious

Thus, when I am referring to several authors at the same time, I will combine their terms when they seem to be referring to the same thing: for example, "subliminal/ subconscious," and so forth.

4. For example, psychiatrist Adolf Meyer found the book hard to read and also found it incredible that Jastrow could blithely ignore the work of Freud, Prince, and Janet (Joseph Jastrow, The Subconscious [Boston: Houghton, Mifflin, 1906]; Adolf Meyer, review of Jastrow [1906], Journal of Philosophy, Psychology, and Scientific Method 4 [1907]:79-82. William Sandy, a British divine, complained that "the style is painful," (Sandy, Christologies Ancient and Modern [Oxford: Clarendon Press, 1910], p.141). Recognizing that, metaphors and all, Jastrow sought to vanquish the concept of the subliminal, fellow psychologist James R. Angell did his best to write an encouraging review (Angell, review of Jastrow [1906], Dial 41 [1906]:106). Jastrow, Professor of Psychology at the University of Wisconsin from 1888 to 1927, later had the audacity to write a scathing critique of psychoanalysis based almost entirely on secondary works (Joseph Jastrow, The House that Freud Built [New York: Greenberg, 1932]; David Shakow and David Rapaport, The Influence of Freud on American Psychology [New York: International Universities Press, 1964], pp.91, 92, 92n, 163, 164). As an experimentalist and dogmatic popularizer, Jastrow unfortunately symbolized, and thus stigmatized, American academic psychology, some of whose practitioners at least were sympathetic to dynamic views.

5. William James, The Varieties of Religious Experience: A Study in Human Nature (New York: Longmans, Green, 1902), p.233.

6. In disagreement with Edmund Gurney's use of the concept of telepathy to explain these psychical phenomena, Myers suggested in this early note "that the right way of regarding these startling incidents is not as isolated psychical operations, but rather as emergent manifestations of psychical operations which are continuous, though latent; and which belong, not so much to the self of which we are habitually conscious, as to a hidden chain of mentation, which, for aught we know, may comprise a continuity of supernormal percipience or activity" (Frederic W. H. Myers, "Note on a Suggested Mode of Psychical Interaction," in Edmund Gurney, Frederic W. H. Myers, and Frank Podmore, Phantasms of the Living [London: Trubner, 1886], 2:277-316, especially p.312). Other comments in James seem to make it clear that in singling out the year 1886 he meant to refer to Phantasms of the Living, and that he intended to focus on Myers' rather than on Gurney's theory, but James could have better chosen either the year 1885 or the year 1891. In this earlier year, Myers published accounts of the "superconscious" and the "super-normal" that were no more vague than his "Note" of 1886 (Myers, "Automatic Writing, or the Rationale of Planchette," Contemporary Review 47 [1885]: 233-249, p.234). Myers does not seem to have found a satisfactory term – "subliminal" – until 1891 (Myers, "The Subliminal Consciousness," Proceedings of the Society for Psychical Research 7 [1891]: 298-355, pp.23, 24, 27, 30).

7. It is curious that Hale also makes a point of the year 1886, but he notes it as the year Janet put forth a specific hypothesis to explain how subjects could obey a posthypnotic suggestion to do something at a designated time in the future. While placing his emphasis on Janet, Hale first explains, "It was as if, 'subconsciously,' something inside the subject were keeping careful count of time," then he suggests that "Janet borrowed this 'self' from F. W. H. Myers" (Hale, Freud and the Americans, pp.126-127).

8. Frederic W. H. Myers, Human Personality and Its Survival of Bodily Death (1903), ed, and abrid. Leopold Myers (London: Longmans, Green, 1906), p.14. Though the idea of the subliminal dates back to Leibnitz, Herbart clarified it, and Fechner developed it to the greatest extent. For a summary statement of the history, see Edwin C. Boring, A

History of Experimental Psychology, 2nd ed. (New York: Appleton-Century-Crofts, 1950), p.639. Although he ends the story around 1880, see also Lancelot Law Whyte, The Unconscious Before Freud (New York: Basic Books, 1960), pp.99, 100, 143, 160-162. Note that in these earlier conceptions of the subliminal the sensations remain unconscious because of their *weakness*.

9. Myers, Human Personality (1903, 1906), p.15.

10. Myers, "Subliminal Consciousness," p.301. Alan Gauld (The Founders of Psychical Research [New York: Schocken, 1968], p.278) objects to explanations of Myers' subliminal that portray it "as a sort of prototype of Jung's 'Analytical psychology'." After characterizing Freud's and Jung's theories as ones in which " 'mental events' move into or out of the searchlight of consciousness," Gauld points out in contrast that Myers "rejected the view that there can be such literally unconscious events". Apparently Gauld fears, as did Myers, that to describe mental events as unconscious is to assign them secondary status and to consign them to oblivion. Thus, he holds fast to Myers' judgment that "for all which lies below that threshold *subliminal* seems the fittest word. 'Unconscious,' or even 'Subconscious,' would be directly misleading". Any word with the prefix "un" tends toward a negative connotation, and thus Myers' "subliminal" would seem the better word, but Freud no less than Myers considered the subliminal/ unconscious primary. Thus, Gauld's objection, insofar as it includes Freud, seems based on a misunderstanding. Freud rejected the word "subconscious" for reasons similar to Myers (see Sigmund Freud, "The Unconscious" [1915], in The Standard Edition of the Complete Psychological Works of Sigmund Freud, ed. James Strachey [London: Hogarth, 1953-1974], 14: 166-204, p.170, and Sigmund Freud, The Question of Lay Analysis: Conversations with an Impartial Person [1926], in Standard Edition, 20: 183-258, p.198).

11. J. Milne Bramwell, Hypnotism: Its History, Practice, and Theory (1903), 3rd ed. (London: W. Rider, 1913), p.437.

12. Frederic W. H. Myers, pp.100-110 under "The British Medical Association and Hypnotism," Proceedings of the Society for Psychical Research 14 (1898): 98-110, p.102.

13. Bramwell, Hypnotism (1903, 1913), p.358.

14. Ibid., p.35.

15. James M. Baldwin, Handbook of Psychology: Volume I: Senses and Intellect (New York: Holt, 1889), p.56.

16. Edward B. Titchener, A Beginner's Psychology (New York: Macmillan, 1915), p.326.

17. James R. Angell, Psychology: An Introductory Study of the Structure and Function of the Human Consciousness, 4th ed. (New York: Holt, 1908), p.455. Most psychology texts discussed this in the chapter on "Attention". Compare George F. Stout (Analytical Psychology [New York: Macmillan, 1896], 1:24) who spoke of "sub-conscious presentations" as "as system of persisting modifications of consciousness of so extremely low a degree of intensity that they have no appreciable power to influence the direction of attention".

18. Titchener, Beginner's Psychology, p.328.

19. Pierre Janet, chapter in Hugo Münsterberg et al, Subconscious Phenomena (Boston: Badger, 1910), pp.53-70, p.62. Despite his dislike of it, Janet nevertheless claimed that he had coined the term "subconscious" (Henri Ellenberger, The Discovery of the Unconscious: The History and Evolution of Dynamic Psychiatry [New York: Basic Books, 1970], p.412, n.82). Apparently, Janet considered this another sign that he had foreshadowed psychoanalysis. For Janet's abusive critique of Freud see Janet, "Psychoanalysis," Journal of Abnormal Psychology 9 (1914): 1-35, 153-187, especially p.35, along with the rejoinder by Ernest Jones, "Professor Janet on Psychoanalysis: A Rejoinder," Journal of Abnormal Psychology 9 (1915): 400-410.

20. Morton Prince, The Dissociation of a Personality: A Biographical Study in Abnormal Psychology (New York: Longmans, Green, 1906), p.530.

21. Boris Sidis, The Psychology of Suggestion: A Research into the Subconscious Nature of Man and Society (New York: Appleton, 1898), pp.89, 128. Boris Sidis and Simon Goodhart, Multiple Personality: An Experimental Investigation into the Nature of Human Individuality (New York: Appleton, 1925), p.49.

22. Pierre Janet, Psychological Healing: A Historical and Clinical Study [1919] (New York: Macmillan, 1925), p.238. Pierre Janet,

Principles of Psychotherapy (New York: Macmillan, 1924), 1:40. According to Ernest Jones (The Life and Work of Sigmund Freud [New York: Basic Books, 1953, 1954, 1957], 1:274 [page 164 in the original:] Freud only "half-heartedly subscribed" to Janet's "dissociation theory" in the "Preliminary Communication" coauthored with Josef Breuer ("On the Psychical Mechanism of Hysterical Phenomena: Preliminary Communication" [1893], Standard Edition, 2: 3-17, p.12). Even Breuer, who seemed to favor the theory ("that 'the splitting of psychical activity ... is present to a *rudimentary* degree in every *major* hysteria' " (Studies on Hysteria [1895], Standard Edition, 2:1-305, p.227. italics mine; the word "major" is not in the version of 1893 cited above), rejected Janet's simplistic account ("It is not the case that the splitting of consciousness occurs because the patients are weak-minded; they appear weak-minded because their mental activity is divided. ... In complete opposition to Janet's views, I believe that ... what underlies dissociation is an excess of efficiency, the habitual co-existence of two heterogeneous trains of ideas" (Breuer and Freud, Studies on Hysteria, pp.231, 233). As early as 1895 Freud left no doubt that he denied Janet's views that hysteria is the result of psychical weakness, inefficiency, and incapacity (Breuer and Freud, Studies on Hysteria, p.104), and he repeated this denial on numerous occasions, including his visit to the United States in 1909 (Five Lectures on Psycho-Analysis [1909], "Second Lecture," Standard Edition, 11:21-28, p.22; "A Short Account of Psycho-Analysis" [1924], Standard Edition, 19:191-209, p.193; see also "Hysteria" [1888], Standard Edition, 1:41-57, p.53 0. Interestingly enough, the first account in English of the "Preliminary Communication," by Myers, focused explicitly on Breuer and Freud's comment that " 'among hysterics we find the clearest-minded, the strongest-willed, the fullest of character, the most acutely critical specimens of humanity' " (Proceedings of the Society for Psychical Research 9 [1893]: 3-25, p.7; Breuer and Freud, "Preliminary Communication" [1893], p.13; Breuer and Freud, Studies on Hysteria, p.232). Nevertheless, Hale (Freud and the Americans, p.128) suggests that Breuer and Freud's "Preliminary Communication" "confirmed Janet's findings that dissociation [the result of psychical weakness] was the 'basic phenomenon' of hysteria".

23. Pierre Janet, The Major Symptoms of Hysteria (1907), 2nd ed. (New York: Macmillan, 1920), p.297.

24. Morton Prince, The Unconscious: The Fundamentals of Human Personality (New York: Macmillan, 1914), p.256.

25. Sidis, Psychology of Suggestion, p.180.

26. Myers, Human Personality (1903, 1906), p.151.

27. Janet, in Münsterberg et al., Subconscious Phenomena, p.62.

28. Boris Sidis, Symptomatology, Psychognosis, and Diagnosis of Psychopathic Diseases (Boston: Badger, 1914), p.x.

29. W. S. Taylor, Morton Prince and Abnormal Psychology (New York: Appleton, 1928), pp.42-43.

30. Jones, Life and Work (1953-1957), 1:250.

31. Myers, Human Personality (1903, 1906, pp.50-55, with reference to Breuer and Freud, Studies on Hysteria, pp.21-47, 106-124. Interestingly enough, both Prince and Sidis were also first attracted to their lives' work through publications on psychical research. Prince: "It was through reading Edmund Gurney's reports on his experiments with hypnotism that my attention was first called to the importance of studying subconscious mental states ...."; Sidis: "My interest in psychopathology dates from the day I became acquainted with Frederic W. H. Myers' preliminary studies of the subconscious (both quotes from H. Addington Bruce, Scientific Mental Healing [Boston: Little, Brown, 1911], p.196).

32. Ernest Jones, Papers on Psycho-Analysis (1914), 3rd ed. (London: Bailliere, Tindall, & Cox, 1923), p.146.

33. Sigmund Freud, "A Note on the Unconscious in Psycho-Analysis" (1912), Standard Edition, 12:260-266; also Proceedings of the Society for Psychical Research 26 (1912): 312-318. Freud had been an honorary member of the Society for Psychical Research since early 1911 (Jones, Life and Work [1953-1957], 2:88).

34. On Fechner and Freud see Henri Ellenberger, "Fechner and Freud," Bulletin of the Menninger Clinic 20 (1956): 201-214; Ellenberger, Discovery of the Unconscious, pp.218, 289, 312, 313, 478, 479, 546; Dieter Wys, Psychoanalytic Schools: From the Beginning to the Present (1961), (New York: Jason Aronson, 1973), pp.97-99; and Jones, Life and Work (1953-1957), 1:372-374.

35. Freud, "A Note on the Unconscious," p.262.

36. Sigmund Freud, The Interpretation of Dreams (1900), Standard Edition, 4:1-338, 5:339-621, p.612; Sigmund Freud, "The Resistances to Psycho-Analysis" (1925), Standard Edition, 19:213-222, p.216; Sigmund Freud, "Some Elementary Lessons in Psycho-Analysis" (1940), Standard Edition, 23:281-286, p.283; Sigmund Freud, The Ego and the Id (1923), Standard Edition, 19:12-59, p.16, n.1.

37. Freud, Interpretation of Dreams, pp.612-613.

38. Morton Prince, introduction and chapter in Münsterberg et al, Subconscious Phenomena, pp.9-15, 71-101, especially pp.10-15, 71.

39. Hartley B. Alexander, "The Subconscious in the Light of Dream Imagery and Imaginative Expression: With Introspective Data," Proceedings of the American Society for Psychical Research 3 (1909): 614-698, pp.614-616. [page 165 in the original:]

40. William James, "Frederic W. H. Myers's Service to Psychology," Popular Science 59 (1901): 380-389, pp.383-385.

41. To this point see Lightner Witmer, "Mental Healing and the Emmanuel Movement (Conclusion)," Psychological Clinic 2 (1908): 282-300, pp.296-299, and James Hyslop, "Religion and Medicine," Journal of the American Society for Psychical Research 2 (1908): 651-681. Worcester certainly held a low opinion of the theories proposed by Janet and Sidis. Concerning the theory that the subconscious is a pathological phenomenon, the psychical concomitant of hysteria, Worcester commented, "Janet came to this conclusion as did Charcot before him from a too limited induction of the facts in question" (Elwood Worcester, Samuel McComb, and Isador Coriat, Religion and Medicine: The Moral Control of Nervous Disorders [New York: Moffat, Yard, 1908], p.41). Worcester and McComb both scoffed at Janet's assertion that only hysterics could be hypnotized, and Worcester quotes Bramwell in ridicule of Sidis' attempt to explain dissociation as the result of minute nerve cell fiber contractions (Worcester, McComb, and Coriat, Religion and Medicine, pp.42, 287, 87). In view of Worcester's unveiled opinion of Janet's views, it is difficult to understand how John Gardner Green ("The Emmanuel Movement: 1906-1929," New England Quarterly Journal 7

[1934]: 495-532, p.518) could refer to <u>Religion and Medicine</u> as an exposition of Janet's doctrines.

42. Elwood Worcester, <u>Life's Adventure: The Story of a Varied Career</u> (New York: Scribner, 1932), pp.277-279.

43. Ibid., pp.287, 87.

44. Ralph Perry, <u>Philosophy of the Recent Past: An Outline of European and American Philosophy Since 1860</u> (New York: Scribner, 1926), pp.85-86.

45. Walter Lowrie, ed., <u>Religion of a Scientist: Selections from Gustav Th. Fechner</u> (New York: Pantheon, 1946), p.47.

46. Elwood Worcester, <u>The Living Word</u> (New York: Moffat, Yard, 1908). To further catch the spirit of Fechner's work see G. Stanley Hall, <u>Founders of Modern Psychology</u> (New York: Appleton, 1912), pp.157-158, and William James, "Concerning Fechner," in <u>A Pluralistic Universe</u> (London: Longmans, Green, 1909), pp.133-177.

47. Lowrie, <u>Religion of a Scientist</u>, p.47.

48. Advertisement, Topeka Journal, 17 December 1908, in scrapbook held by Dr. Blandina Worcester, Ridgefield, Conn.

49. One important place they differed was in their concept of the soul. Whereas Worcester, following Fechner, saw the subliminal/subconscious as the soul, Myers conceived the soul as a broader unifying continuum of which the supra- and subliminal were two modifications. See Gauld, <u>Psychical Research</u>, p.301.

50. [Elwood Worcester and Samuel McComb], "The Health Conference," <u>in Emmanuel Parish Year Book</u> (Boston: Emmanuel Church, 1907), pp.62-63; Worcester, McComb, and Coriat, <u>Religion and Medicine</u>, p.42.

51. Ibid., pp.26, 29, 63, 35, 19, 42.

52. Hugo Münsterberg, <u>Psychotherapy</u> (New York: Moffat, Yard, 1909), p.125; American Medicine 15 (1909): 599.

53. See Powell, <u>Healing and Wholeness</u>, pp.187-190.

54. Hibbert Journal (Jan.1909): 295-313, 278-294, 241-260, 261-277.

55. American Journal of Theology (1909): 337-349; George B. Cutten, Psychological Phenomena of Christianity (London: Hodder & Stoughton, 1909), p.18.

56. Edwin D. Starbuck, Psychology of Religion: An Empirical Study of the Growth of Religious Consciousness (New York: Scribner, 1899).

57. Hibbert Journal (1903-1904): 44-64, 514-531; George T. Ladd, The Philosophy of Religion: A Critical and Speculative Treatise on Man's Religious Experience and Development in the Light of Modern Science and Reflective Thinking (New York: Scribner, 1905), 1:266.

58. Sanday, Christologies, p.159.

59. Shakow and Rapaport, Influence of Freud, p.8.

60. Ibid., p.107.

#

&&&

The Author's Comments in 2015:

This research originally was presented before the Josiah C. Macy Seminar on the History of Medicine and the Biological Sciences, Princeton, NJ, March 1974.

This article originally was published in the Journal of the History of the Behavioral Sciences 15: 155-165, 1979.

The opening abstract was not originally in italics.

The original starting place of each page of text is indicated, so that previous citations of this article still will be accurate.

The manuscript began as a footnote to my doctoral dissertation – a footnote that became longer and longer and longer until one of my dissertation advisors, Seymour Mauskopf, PhD (1938-   ) suggested that it be spun off as an article. As noted at the bottom of the first page of the original publication, "This article was written (1973) during the tenure (1968-1974) of a predoctoral fellowship in the history of medicine and biological sciences from the Josiah Macy, Jr. Foundation, New York". It further was noted that "Robert Charles Powell received his MD and PhD (history) degrees from Duke University, Durham, North Carolina, in 1974. At the time this manuscript was accepted, he held positions as Resident in Psychiatry, Upstate Medical Center, State University of New York at Syracuse, and Assistant Professor of History, University of Missouri-Kansas City".

One can argue the pros and cons of changing the 1979

custom of using male pronouns and nouns when reference most likely is to both men and women. The decision here has been to augment "laymen" with "{/laywomen}," "laymen's" with "{/laywomen's}," "clergyman" with "{/clergywoman}," "he" with {/she}"; the goal here has been to keep the original text intact while signaling what might be a reasonable way to proceed if reading that portion of the text out loud.

One can argue the pros and cons of changing the 1979 usage of spelling "G-d" with the "o" intact. The decision here has been to take the most conservative path, considering that leaving out one letter maintains the meaning while reducing the chance that a sacred name might be profaned; technically, the original guidance for taking this approach applied only within certain vulnerable areas of Hebrew writing.

While the original text did not underscore book titles, that is done here. While the original text placed articles' dates of publication in parentheses after the volume number – a pattern now not generally followed – that approach is maintained here. Whenever a few quoted words fall at the end of a sentence, the period has been placed outside of the quotation mark rather than inside, as had been done in the original text. In the endnotes, colons after authors' names have been replaced with commas. The first manuscript retains the spelling "Leipsic" and the second manuscript retains the word "Leipzig"; apparently the argument has been going on for over two centuries as to the correct spelling and I have chosen not to join the fray. Cutten's Psychological Phenomena of Christianity (mentioned on page 161) apparently was published in both 1908 and 1909 without any indication of there being separate editions; this manuscript's original use of the date of 1909 has been kept while here signaling that the date of 1908 also is correct. The following other minor changes have been made to the text: p.155: "Freud and the Americans" has been replaced with "Freud and the Americans ..."; "James's Varieties of Religious Experience" has been replaced with "James' Varieties of Religious Experience ..."; "Human Personality" has been replaced with "Human Personality ..."; "Hypnotism" has been replaced with "Hypnotism ..."; p.156: "Religion and Medicine" has been replaced with "Religion and

Medicine ..."; p.159: "was widely held" has been replaced with "was held widely"; "can be clearly seen" has been replaced with "can be seen clearly"; p.160: "he was still feeling" has been replaced with "he still was feeling"; "could just as well be" has been replaced with "just as well could be"; again, "Religion and Medicine" has been replaced with "Religion and Medicine ..."; p.161: "Psychology of Religion" has been replaced with "Psychology of Religion ..."; p.162: "Ann Arbor: Xerox University Microfilms, # 75-2415" has been replaced with "Ann Arbor: ProQuest (order # AAT 7502415)"; "Recog-" (an obvious typographic error) has been replaced with "Recognizing"; "were at least sympathetic" has been replaced by "at least were sympathetic"; in note 3,underscoring has been added; p.163: "Subconscious Phenomena (Boston: Badger, 1910), pp.53-70, 62" has been replaced with "Subconscious Phenomena (Boston: Badger, 1910), pp.53-70, p.62"; p.164: "Mechanism of Histerical Phenomena" has been replaced with "Mechanism of Hysterical Phenomena"; "London: L. Bailliere, Tindall, & Cox" has been replaced with "London: Bailliere, Tindall, & Cox";

Extra Endnotes

Endnote 1: At the time this manuscript was written, only the first volume of Hale's Freud and the Americans: The Beginnings of Psychoanalysis in the United States, 1876-1917 (1971) had been published. Over two decades later Hale's The Rise and Crisis of Psychoanalysis in the United States: Freud and the Americans, 1917-1985 (1995) appeared. Most reviewers recognized this as essentially a two-volume set. While Hale's hard work must be acknowledged, there were problems with his research. I wrote one of the few truly critical reviews of the "first volume": "one must ask why he has allowed himself to comment on some topics that he doesn't seem to have personally explored. ... Such partial acquaintance with the easily accessible psychiatric literature may tend to confuse those readers not at home in the field. ... Finally, one wonders how Professor Hale justifies the presentistic comments on psychiatry and psychoanalysis that pepper his predominantly historical narrative." [Bulletin of the History of Medicine 50: 144-145, 1976] I was chastised by the chair of my dissertation committee, "Don't you know he has cancer?" – as if that fact should have made me soften my review. (I did not know. Nathan G. Hale, Jr, born in 1922 "passed away peacefully in his sleep" in 2013, according to his obituary.) The chastiser further noted that he had apologized to Hale for the harshness of my review! Four years later a scathing review of a Hale article made observations similar to mine: "He must not be permitted … to state such interpretations as if they were facts and it is even worse if he has not checked their accuracy. … It must be taken for granted that the author never saw the volume about which he made such a derogatory remark. … In conclusion, it is regrettable that an historian so highly esteemed … makes judgments over matters he has not cared to study." [Ernst Federn – "On the Difficulty of Writing History of Ideas: A Reply." Journal of the History of the Behavioral Sciences 16(1): 45-49, 1980].

Endnote 2: As indicated (somewhat cryptically) in the original endnotes, I was the one who discovered the "Worcester Papers" in 1973. On a cold, snowy day, going systematically down a list of known theological depositories in the Boston area, I finally got to my eleventh and last stop, the Episcopal Diocesan Library. I presented my letter of introduction to the Registrar, Mr. Harley P. Holden, mentioning that I was looking for the papers of the Rev. Dr. Elwood Ernest Worcester. Mr. Holden just sat there, as if in a trance, staring at my letter. Then he asked, "What was that name again – the name of the man whose papers you are seeking?" "Elwood E. Worcester," I replied. Again, Mr. Holden just sat there staring at my letter. Suddenly he stood up, saying, "Come with me," as he scurried up the stairs until we arrived in what seemed to be the attic of the building. There in the middle of the well-lighted, handsomely carpeted room lay a burst open steamer trunk with manuscripts spilling out everywhere. Apparently workers, still seen milling around, repairing attic eaves, had come across this heavy trunk full of Worcester's papers. Someone must have told the registrar of the trunk, but, clearly, no one had investigated further. As bizarre as this might seem, I sat on the floor and began taking notes about the manuscripts that had been hidden away for decades. When the diocesan library closed, I returned to the Rare Books Room of the Countway Library of Medicine, where I had left my belongings and which was just about to close for the day. Telling the librarian, Mr. Richard Wolfe, of my discovery, he immediately flipped the lights back on and phoned Mr. Holden, who, I now learned, just happened also to be the Curator of the Harvard University Archives. Apparently the "Worcester Papers" got whisked from the diocesan attic and to the university, because that is where they are today – without any mention of how they had been found just hours before a young scholar came looking for them. Perhaps Worcester's spirit guided the events of that day.

Endnote 7: This one sentence, concerning which 1886 item influenced William James' notion of the subconscious – and to which he dated the dawn of modern psychology – has been cited extensively by others. Among the more insightful commentators has been Adam Crabtree, in a footnote on page 301 of his chapter in Kelly, Edward F. et al, Irreducible Mind: Toward a Psychology for the 21st Century, Lanham, MD: Rowman & Littlefield, 2006; seven authors' conclusions were discarded by Crabtree and the current article's conclusion was accepted.

Endnote 48: While "Blandina Rulison Worcester" (1902-1984) was her baptismal name, her oldest son noted that he believed her father, when she was in high school or college, encouraged her to use another maternal family name, "Van Antwerp," instead of the maternal family name "Rulison". Professionally, she referred to herself as "Blandina Van A. Worcester, MD" or as "Blandina Worcester, MD". Socially, she referred to herself as "Mrs. Carroll H. Brewster" or as "Blandina W. Brewster". During 1973 I spoke with her once by chance at her youngest son's home in Ithaca, and once by chance at her sister's (and parents') home in Boston, and once by appointment at her Ridgefield farm. Her oldest son, Carroll H. Brewster, now resides on the farm in Ridgefield, CT; the scrapbook was last seen there by the family but is not currently located.

Since the first appearance of this article, the following relevant studies have been published:

Alvarado, Carlos S., "Historical Writings on Parapsychology and Its Contributions to Psychology," Psypioneer 1(20): 270-274, 2005.

http://www.woodlandway.org/PDF/20.PSYPIONEERFoundedbyLeslieP
rice.pdf ; also found at Parapsychological Association e-newsletter Winter
2003.
http://archived.parapsych.org/newsletters/pa_newsletter_winter2003.htm
l

Brottman, Mikita, <u>Phantoms of the Clinic: From Thought-Transference to Projective Identification</u>. London: Karnac Books, 2011.

The following relevant study from the past was discovered:

Troland, Leonard T., "The Freudian psychology and psychical research," The Journal of Abnormal Psychology 8(6):405-428, 1914.
#

Also by
Robert Charles Powell

ANTON T.
BOISEN
(1876-1965)
:
*"Breaking an Opening in
the Wall between
Religion and Medicine"*

ANTON T.
BOISEN
(1876-1965)
:
*"Cooperative Inquiry":
"Amid the Complex
Entanglements of
Actual Life"*

ANTON T.
BOISEN
(1876-1965)
:
*Studying Empirically
"the Complex
Entanglements of
Actual Life"*

ANTON T.
BOISEN
(1876-1965)
:
CLINICIAN
:
*A Guide to Clinical Pastoral
Assessment & Therapy*

THE
CLINICAL
PASTORAL
MOVEMENT
:
The First
*Fifty Years of Learning
through Supervised
Encounter
with "Living Human
Documents"*
(1925-1975)
&
some thoughts about
the second fifty years
(1975-2025)

PSYCHOSOMATIC
HEALING
& CLINICAL
PASTORAL CARE
:
*an Holistic, Organismic,
Dantean, Devotional
Approach*
:
The Contributions of
Helen Flanders Dunbar

FREUDIAN
CONCEPTS IN
AMERICA:
*The Role of
Psychical Research in
Preparing the Way:
1904-1934*

WHEN DEATH
IS NOT
THEORETICAL:
*The Readiness of the Music
Group 'Queen' for
Living with Freddie
Mercury's Dying*

www.ingramcontent.com/pod-product-compliance
Lightning Source LLC
Chambersburg PA
CBHW030540290526
45786CB00004B/1790